CONTENTS

PHILLY Fresh Mediterranean Dip

Prep: 10 min. **Makes:** 1¾ cups or 14 servings, 2 Tbsp. each.

- 1 pkg. (8 oz.) **PHILADELPHIA** Neufchâtel Cheese, ⅓ Less Fat than Cream Cheese, softened
- ½ cup chopped tomato
- ½ cup chopped cucumbers
- ½ cup chopped spinach leaves
- ¼ cup chopped red onions
- 2 Tbsp. **KRAFT** Greek Vinaigrette Dressing
- ¼ cup **ATHENOS** Crumbled Feta Cheese with Basil & Tomato

SPREAD Neufchâtel cheese onto bottom of 9-inch pie plate.

MIX remaining ingredients except feta cheese; spoon over Neufchâtel cheese. Sprinkle with feta cheese.

SERVE with WHEAT THINS Snack Crackers or assorted cut-up fresh vegetables.

PHILADELPHIA

Easy Entertaining

PHILLY BBQ Ranch Chicken Dip

Prep: 10 min. **Makes:** 2¼ cups or 18 servings, 2 Tbsp. each.

1 pkg. (8 oz.) **PHILADELPHIA** Neufchâtel Cheese, ⅓ Less Fat than Cream Cheese, softened

¼ cup **KRAFT** Barbecue Sauce, any flavor

1 pkg. (6 oz.) **OSCAR MAYER** Grilled Chicken Breast Strips, chopped

2 Tbsp. **KRAFT** Light Ranch Reduced Fat Dressing

¼ cup chopped red bell pepper

¼ cup sliced green onions

SPREAD Neufchâtel cheese onto bottom of microwaveable 9-inch pie plate. Spread barbecue sauce over Neufchâtel cheese. Top with chicken.

MICROWAVE on HIGH 2 min. or until heated through. Top with remaining ingredients.

SERVE with WHEAT THINS Snack Crackers and cut up vegetables.

PHILADELPHIA

Easy Entertaining

PHILLY Cheesy Chili Dip

Prep: 5 min. **Makes:** 3 cups or 24 servings, 2 Tbsp. each.

- 1 pkg. (8 oz.) **PHILADELPHIA** Cream Cheese, softened
- 1 can (15 oz.) chili
- ½ cup **KRAFT** Shredded Cheddar Cheese
- 2 Tbsp. chopped cilantro

SPREAD cream cheese onto bottom of microwaveable pie plate; top with chili and Cheddar cheese.

MICROWAVE on HIGH 45 sec. to 1 min. or until Cheddar cheese is melted. Sprinkle with cilantro.

SERVE with assorted NABISCO Crackers.

Easy Entertaining

PHILADELPHIA Mexican Dip

Prep: 10 min. **Makes:** 1⅔ cups dip or 13 servings, 2 Tbsp. dip and 16 crackers each.

1 pkg. (8 oz.) **PHILADELPHIA** Neufchâtel Cheese, ⅓ Less Fat than Cream Cheese, softened

½ cup **TACO BELL® HOME ORIGINALS®** Thick 'N Chunky Salsa

½ cup **KRAFT** 2% Milk Shredded Reduced Fat Cheddar Cheese

2 green onions, sliced (about ¼ cup)

WHEAT THINS Reduced Fat Baked Snack Crackers

SPREAD Neufchâtel cheese onto bottom of 9-inch pie plate.

TOP with layers of salsa, Cheddar cheese and onions.

SERVE with the crackers.

TACO BELL® and HOME ORIGINALS® are trademarks owned and licensed by Taco Bell Corp.

Heavenly Ham Roll-Ups

Prep: 15 min. **Bake:** 20 min. **Makes:** 15 servings, 1 roll-up each.

1 pkg. (9 oz.) **OSCAR MAYER** Shaved Smoked Ham
5 Tbsp. **PHILADELPHIA** Light Cream Cheese Spread
15 asparagus spears (about 1 lb.), trimmed

PREHEAT oven to 350°F. Flatten ham slices; pat dry. Stack ham in piles of 2 slices each; spread each stack with 1 tsp. of the cream cheese spread.

PLACE 1 asparagus spear on one of the long sides of each ham stack; roll up. Place in 13×9-inch baking dish.

BAKE 15 to 20 min. or until heated through.

Easy Entertaining

Savory Bruschetta

Prep: 15 min. **Bake:** 10 min. **Makes:** 24 servings, 1 slice each.

¼ cup olive oil

1 clove garlic, minced

1 loaf (1 lb.) French bread, cut in half lengthwise

1 pkg. (8 oz.) **PHILADELPHIA** Cream Cheese, softened

3 Tbsp. **KRAFT** 100% Grated Parmesan Cheese

2 Tbsp. chopped pitted ripe olives

1 cup chopped plum tomatoes

¼ cup chopped fresh basil

PREHEAT oven to 400°F. Mix oil and garlic; spread onto cut surfaces of bread. Bake 8 to 10 min. or until lightly browned. Cool.

MIX cream cheese and Parmesan cheese with electric mixer on medium speed until blended. Stir in olives.

SPREAD toasted bread halves with cream cheese mixture; top with tomatoes. Cut into 24 slices to serve. Sprinkle with basil.

Easy Entertaining

Pecan Tassies

Prep: 20 min. plus refrigerating. **Bake:** 25 min. **Makes:** 2 dozen or 24 servings, 1 tart each.

- 4 oz. (½ of 8-oz. pkg.) **PHILADELPHIA** Cream Cheese, softened
- ½ cup (1 stick) butter or margarine, softened
- 1 cup all-purpose flour
- 1 egg
- ¾ cup firmly packed brown sugar
- 1 tsp. vanilla
- ¾ cup finely chopped **PLANTERS** Pecans
- 3 squares **BAKER'S** Semi-Sweet Baking Chocolate, melted

BEAT cream cheese and butter in large bowl with electric mixer on medium speed until well blended. Add flour; mix well. Cover and refrigerate at least 1 hour or until chilled.

PREHEAT oven to 350°F. Divide dough into 24 balls. Place 1 ball in each of 24 miniature muffin pan cups; press onto bottoms and up sides of cups to form shells. Set aside. Beat egg lightly in small bowl. Add sugar and vanilla; mix well. Stir in pecans. Spoon evenly into pastry shells, filling each shell three-fourths full.

BAKE 25 min. or until lightly browned. Let stand 5 min. in pans; remove to wire racks. Cool completely. Drizzle with melted chocolate. Let stand until set.

PHILADELPHIA

Easy Entertaining

Easy Petit Fours

Prep: 5 min. **Makes:** 12 servings.

¼ cup **PHILADELPHIA** Strawberry Cream Cheese Spread
12 **OREO** White Fudge Covered Chocolate Sandwich Cookies
 6 strawberries, halved
 1 square **BAKER'S** Semi-Sweet Baking Chocolate, melted

SPREAD 1 tsp. cream cheese onto each cookie. Top each with strawberry half.

DRIZZLE each strawberry-topped cookie with melted chocolate.

Easy Entertaining

Cream Cheese Nibbles

Prep: 10 min. plus refrigerating. **Makes:** 18 servings, 2 pieces each.

- 1 pkg. (8 oz.) **PHILADELPHIA** Cream Cheese
- ½ cup **KRAFT** Sun-Dried Tomato Dressing
- 2 cloves garlic, sliced
- 3 small sprigs fresh rosemary, stems removed
- 6 sprigs fresh thyme, cut into pieces
- 1 tsp. black peppercorns
  Peel of 1 lemon, cut into thin strips

CUT cream cheese into 36 pieces. Place in 9-inch pie plate.

ADD remaining ingredients; toss lightly. Cover.

REFRIGERATE at least 1 hour or up to 24 hours. Serve with crusty bread, NABISCO Crackers or pita chips.

PHILADELPHIA

Classic Cheesecakes

Tiramisu Cheesecake

Prep: 20 min. plus refrigerating. **Bake:** 45 min. **Makes:** 16 servings, 1 piece each.

- 1 box (12 oz.) **NILLA** Wafers (about 88 wafers), divided
- 5 tsp. **MAXWELL HOUSE** Instant Coffee, divided
- 3 Tbsp. hot water, divided
- 4 pkg. (8 oz. each) **PHILADELPHIA** Cream Cheese, softened
- 1 cup sugar
- 1 cup **BREAKSTONE'S** or **KNUDSEN** Sour Cream
- 4 eggs
- 1 cup thawed **COOL WHIP** Whipped Topping
- 2 Tbsp. unsweetened cocoa powder

PREHEAT oven to 325°F. Line 13×9-inch baking pan with foil, with ends of foil extending over sides of pan. Layer half of the wafers (about 44) on bottom of prepared pan. Dissolve 2 tsp. of the coffee granules in 2 Tbsp. of the hot water. Brush wafers with half of the dissolved coffee mixture; set remaining aside.

BEAT cream cheese and sugar in large bowl with electric mixer on medium speed until well blended. Add sour cream; mix well. Add eggs, 1 at a time, mixing on low speed after each addition just until blended. Dissolve remaining 3 tsp. coffee granules in remaining 1 Tbsp. hot water. Remove 3½ cups of the batter; place in medium bowl. Stir in dissolved coffee. Pour coffee-flavored batter over wafers in baking pan. Layer remaining wafers over batter. Brush wafers with reserved dissolved coffee. Pour remaining plain batter over wafers.

BAKE 45 min. or until center is almost set. Cool. Refrigerate 3 hours or overnight. Lift cheesecake from pan, using foil handles. Spread with whipped topping; sprinkle with cocoa. Cut into 16 pieces to serve. Store leftover cheesecake in refrigerator.

Classic Cheesecakes

New York Cheesecake

Prep: 15 min. plus refrigerating. **Bake:** 40 min. **Makes:** 16 servings, 1 slice each.

- 1 cup crushed **HONEY MAID** Honey Grahams (about 6 grahams)
- 3 Tbsp. sugar
- 3 Tbsp. butter or margarine, melted
- 5 pkg. (8 oz. each) **PHILADELPHIA** Cream Cheese, softened
- 1 cup sugar
- 3 Tbsp. all-purpose flour
- 1 Tbsp. vanilla
- 1 cup **BREAKSTONE'S** or **KNUDSEN** Sour Cream
- 4 eggs
- 1 can (21 oz.) cherry pie filling

PREHEAT oven to 325°F. Mix crumbs, 3 Tbsp. of the sugar and butter; press firmly onto bottom of 13×9-inch baking pan. Bake 10 min.

BEAT cream cheese, 1 cup sugar, flour and vanilla with electric mixer on medium speed until well blended. Add sour cream; mix well. Add eggs, 1 at a time, mixing on low speed after each addition just until blended. Pour over crust.

BAKE 40 min. or until center is almost set. Cool completely. Refrigerate at least 4 hours or overnight. Top with pie filling before serving. Store leftover cheesecake in refrigerator.

Jazz It Up: Omit pie filling. Arrange 2 cups mixed berries on top of chilled cheesecake. Brush with 2 Tbsp. melted strawberry jelly.

Our Best Chocolate Cheesecake

Prep: 30 min. plus refrigerating. **Bake:** 55 min. **Makes:** 16 servings.

- 1½ cups crushed **OREO** Chocolate Sandwich Cookies (about 18 cookies)
- 2 Tbsp. butter or margarine, melted
- 3 pkg. (8 oz. each) **PHILADELPHIA** Cream Cheese, softened
- 1 cup sugar
- 1 tsp. vanilla
- 1 pkg. (8 squares) **BAKER'S** Semi-Sweet Baking Chocolate, melted, slightly cooled
- 3 eggs
- 1 cup thawed **COOL WHIP** Strawberry Whipped Topping
- 1½ cups assorted seasonal fruit, such as chopped strawberries and sliced kiwi

PREHEAT oven to 325°F if using a silver 9-inch springform pan (or to 300°F if using a dark nonstick 9-inch springform pan). Mix crushed cookies and butter; press firmly onto bottom of pan. Bake 10 min.

BEAT cream cheese, sugar and vanilla with electric mixer on medium speed until well blended. Add chocolate; mix well. Add eggs, 1 at a time, mixing on low speed after each addition just until blended. Pour over crust.

BAKE 45 to 55 min. or until center is almost set. Run knife or metal spatula around rim of pan to loosen cake; cool before removing rim of pan. Refrigerate 4 hours or overnight. Top with whipped topping and fruit.

How To Soften Cream Cheese: Place completely unwrapped pkg. of cream cheese in microwaveable bowl. Microwave on HIGH 45 sec. or until slightly softened.

PHILADELPHIA

Classic Cheesecakes

Apple Pecan Cheesecake

Prep: 15 min. plus refrigerating. **Bake:** 55 min. **Makes:** 16 servings, 1 piece each.

- 1½ cups **HONEY MAID** Graham Cracker Crumbs
- ¼ cup (½ stick) butter, melted
- 2 Tbsp. firmly packed brown sugar
- 4 pkg. (8 oz. each) **PHILADELPHIA** Cream Cheese, softened
- 1½ cups firmly packed brown sugar, divided
- 1 tsp. vanilla
- 1 cup **BREAKSTONE'S** or **KNUDSEN** Sour Cream
- 4 eggs
- 4 cups chopped peeled apples (about 3 medium)
- ¾ cup **PLANTERS** Chopped Pecans
- 1 tsp. ground cinnamon

PREHEAT oven to 325°F. Line 13×9-inch baking pan with foil, with ends of foil extending over sides of pan. Mix crumbs, butter and 2 Tbsp. brown sugar; press firmly onto bottom of pan.

BEAT cream cheese, 1 cup of the brown sugar and the vanilla in large bowl with electric mixer on medium speed until well blended. Add sour cream; mix well. Add eggs, 1 at a time, mixing on low speed after each addition just until blended. Pour over crust. Mix remaining ½ cup brown sugar, the apples, pecans and cinnamon; spoon evenly over cheesecake batter.

BAKE 55 min. or until center is almost set. Cool. Refrigerate 4 hours or overnight. Let stand at room temperature 30 min. before serving. Lift cheesecake from pan, using foil handles. Cut into 16 pieces. Store leftover cheesecake in refrigerator.

PHILADELPHIA

Classic Cheesecakes

White Chocolate Cheesecake

Prep: 30 min. plus refrigerating. **Bake:** 1 hour. **Makes:** 16 servings.

- ¾ cup sugar, divided
- ½ cup (1 stick) butter, softened
- 1½ tsp. vanilla, divided
- 1 cup all-purpose flour
- 4 pkg. (8 oz. each) **PHILADELPHIA** Cream Cheese, softened
- 2 pkg. (6 squares each) **BAKER'S** Premium White Baking Chocolate, melted, slightly cooled
- 4 eggs
- 1 pt. (2 cups) raspberries

PREHEAT oven to 325°F if using a silver 9-inch springform pan (or to 300°F if using a dark nonstick 9-inch springform pan). Beat ¼ cup of the sugar, the butter and ½ tsp. of the vanilla in small bowl with electric mixer on medium speed until light and fluffy. Gradually add flour, mixing on low speed until well blended after each addition. Press firmly onto bottom of pan; prick with fork. Bake 25 min. or until edge is lightly browned.

BEAT cream cheese, remaining ½ cup sugar and remaining 1 tsp. vanilla in large bowl with electric mixer on medium speed until well blended. Add melted chocolate; mix well. Add eggs, 1 at a time, beating on low speed after each addition just until blended. Pour over crust.

BAKE 55 min. to 1 hour or until center is almost set. Run knife or metal spatula around rim of pan to loosen cake; cool before removing rim of pan. Refrigerate 4 hours or overnight. Top with the raspberries just before serving. Store leftover cheesecake in refrigerator.

Granulated
SUGAR

PHILADELPHIA

Classic Cheesecakes

Triple-Citrus Cheesecake

Prep: 30 min. plus refrigerating. **Bake:** 1 hour 5 min. **Makes:** 16 servings.

- 1 cup **HONEY MAID** Graham Cracker Crumbs
- ⅓ cup firmly packed brown sugar
- ¼ cup (½ stick) butter or margarine, melted
- 4 pkg. (8 oz. each) **PHILADELPHIA** Cream Cheese, softened
- 1 cup granulated sugar
- 2 Tbsp. all-purpose flour
- 1 tsp. vanilla
- 4 eggs
- 1 Tbsp. fresh lemon juice
- 1 Tbsp. fresh lime juice
- 1 Tbsp. fresh orange juice
- 1 tsp. grated lemon peel
- 1 tsp. grated lime peel
- 1 tsp. grated orange peel

PREHEAT oven to 325°F if using a silver 9-inch springform pan (or to 300°F if using a dark nonstick 9-inch springform pan). Mix crumbs, brown sugar and butter; press firmly onto bottom of pan. Bake 10 min.

BEAT cream cheese, granulated sugar, flour and vanilla with electric mixer on medium speed until well blended. Add eggs, 1 at a time, mixing on low speed after each addition just until blended. Stir in remaining ingredients; pour over crust.

BAKE 1 hour 5 min. or until center is almost set. Run knife or metal spatula around rim of pan to loosen cake; cool before removing rim of pan. Refrigerate 4 hours or overnight. Garnish as desired. Store leftover cheesecake in refrigerator.

PHILADELPHIA

Classic Cheesecakes

Ribbon Bar Cheesecake

Prep: 15 min. plus refrigerating. **Bake:** 40 min. **Makes:** 16 servings, 1 square each.

- 30 **OREO** Chocolate Sandwich Cookies, crushed
- ½ cup (1 stick) butter, melted
- ¼ cup **PLANTERS** Chopped Pecans
- ¼ cup **BAKER'S ANGEL FLAKE** Coconut
- 4 pkg. (8 oz. each) **PHILADELPHIA** Cream Cheese, softened
- 1 cup sugar
- 4 eggs
- ½ cup whipping cream
- 6 squares **BAKER'S** Semi-Sweet Baking Chocolate

PREHEAT oven to 350°F. Mix crushed cookies, butter, pecans and coconut; press firmly onto bottom of 13×9-inch baking pan. Refrigerate while preparing filling.

BEAT cream cheese and sugar in large bowl with electric mixer on medium speed until well blended. Add eggs, 1 at a time, mixing on low speed after each addition just until blended. Pour over crust.

BAKE 40 min. or until center is almost set. Cool. Refrigerate 3 hours or overnight. Place whipping cream and chocolate in saucepan. Cook on low heat until chocolate is completely melted and mixture is well blended, stirring occasionally. Pour over cheesecake. Refrigerate 15 min. or until chocolate is firm. Store leftover cheesecake in refrigerator.

PHILADELPHIA New York Cappuccino Cheesecake

Prep: 15 min. plus refrigerating. **Bake:** 1 hour 5 min. **Makes:** 16 servings.

- 1 cup chocolate wafer cookie crumbs
- 3 Tbsp. sugar
- 2 Tbsp. butter or margarine, melted
- 5 pkg. (8 oz. each) **PHILADELPHIA** Cream Cheese, softened
- 1 cup sugar
- 3 Tbsp. all-purpose flour
- 1 Tbsp. vanilla
- 3 eggs
- 1 cup **BREAKSTONE'S** or **KNUDSEN** Sour Cream
- 1 Tbsp. **MAXWELL HOUSE** Instant Coffee
- 3 Tbsp. coffee-flavored liqueur

PREHEAT oven to 350°F if using a silver 9-inch springform pan (or to 325°F if using a dark nonstick 9-inch springform pan). Mix crumbs, 3 Tbsp. sugar and the butter; press firmly onto bottom of pan. Bake 10 min.

BEAT cream cheese, 1 cup sugar, the flour and vanilla in large bowl with electric mixer on medium speed until well blended. Add eggs, 1 at a time, mixing on low speed after each addition just until blended. Add sour cream; mix well. Stir instant coffee granules into liqueur until dissolved. Blend into batter. Pour over crust.

BAKE 1 hour 5 min. or until center is almost set. Run knife or metal spatula around rim of pan to loosen cake; cool before removing rim of pan. Refrigerate 4 hours or overnight. Store leftover cheesecake in refrigerator.

Classic Cheesecakes

PHILADELPHIA Black Forest Cheesecake

Prep: 15 min. plus refrigerating. **Bake:** 40 min. **Makes** 16 servings, 1 piece each.

- 20 **OREO** Chocolate Sandwich Cookies, crushed (about 2 cups)
- 3 Tbsp. butter, melted
- 4 pkg. (8 oz. each) **PHILADELPHIA** Cream Cheese, softened
- 1 cup sugar
- 1 tsp. vanilla
- 1 cup **BREAKSTONE'S** or **KNUDSEN** Sour Cream
- 6 squares **BAKER'S** Semi-Sweet Baking Chocolate, melted
- 4 eggs
- 2 cups thawed **COOL WHIP** Whipped Topping
- 1 can (21 oz.) cherry pie filling

PREHEAT oven to 325°F. Line 13×9-inch baking pan with foil, with ends of foil extending over sides of pan. Mix cookie crumbs and butter; press firmly onto bottom of prepared pan. Bake 10 min.

BEAT cream cheese, sugar and vanilla in large bowl with electric mixer on medium speed until well blended. Add sour cream and chocolate; mix well. Add eggs, 1 at a time, mixing on low speed after each addition just until blended. Pour over crust.

BAKE 40 min. or until center is almost set. Cool. Refrigerate at least 4 hours or overnight. Lift cheesecake from pan, using foil handles. Top with whipped topping and pie filling. Store any leftover cheesecake in refrigerator.

PHILADELPHIA

Seasonal Desserts

Great Pumpkin Cake

Prep: 30 min. **Bake:** As directed. **Makes:** 24 servings, 1 slice each.

- 1 pkg. (2-layer) cake mix, any flavor
- 1 pkg. (8 oz.) **PHILADELPHIA** Cream Cheese, softened
- ¼ cup (½ stick) butter, softened
- 4 cups powdered sugar
  Few drops each: green, red and yellow food coloring
- 1 **COMET** Ice Cream Cone

PREPARE cake batter and bake in 12-cup fluted tube pan as directed on package. Cool in pan 10 min. Invert cake onto wire rack; remove pan. Cool cake completely.

MEANWHILE, beat cream cheese and butter in medium bowl with electric mixer on medium speed until well blended. Gradually add sugar, beating until well blended after each addition. Remove ½ cup of the frosting; place in small bowl. Add green food coloring; stir until well blended. Spread half of the green frosting onto outside of ice cream cone; set aside. Cover and reserve remaining green frosting for later use.

ADD red and yellow food colorings to remaining white frosting to tint it orange. Spread onto cake to resemble pumpkin. Invert ice cream cone in hole in top of cake for the pumpkin's stem. Pipe the reserved green frosting in vertical lines down side of cake.

Cooking Know-How: For a more rounded Great Pumpkin Cake, use a tall 12-cup fluted tube pan. As the cake bakes, it rises and forms a rounded top. When cake is unmolded (upside-down), the bottom of the cake will be rounded. If the cake is baked in a shorter 12-cup fluted tube pan, the resulting cake will be flatter.

PHILADELPHIA

Seasonal Desserts

Rustic Fall Fruit Tart

Prep: 15 min. **Bake:** 30 min. **Makes:** 8 servings.

1½ cups all-purpose flour
½ cup (1 stick) butter, softened
½ cup (½ of 8-oz. container)
   PHILADELPHIA Cream Cheese
   Spread
4 medium plums, thinly sliced
2 medium nectarines, thinly sliced
⅓ cup sugar
1 tsp. ground ginger
1 Tbsp. cornstarch
⅓ cup apricot jam

PLACE flour, butter and cream cheese in food processor container; cover. Process, using pulsing action, until mixture is well blended and almost forms a ball. Shape dough into ball; wrap tightly with plastic wrap. Refrigerate 1 hour or until chilled.

PREHEAT oven to 400°F. Place pastry on lightly floured surface; roll out to 12-inch circle. Place on lightly greased baking sheet; set aside. Toss fruit with sugar, ginger and cornstarch. Arrange decoratively over crust to within 2 inches of edge of crust. Fold edge of crust over fruit.

BAKE 30 min. Remove from oven; spread fruit with jam. Serve warm or at room temperature.

Size It Up: Sweets can add enjoyment to a balanced diet, but choose an appropriate portion.

Spider Web Pumpkin Cheesecake

Prep: 15 min. plus refrigerating. **Bake:** 55 min. **Makes:** 16 servings.

18 **OREO** Chocolate Sandwich Cookies, finely crushed
    (about 1½ cups)
 2 Tbsp. butter or margarine, melted
 3 pkg. (8 oz. each) **PHILADELPHIA** Cream Cheese, softened
¾ cup sugar
 1 can (15 oz.) pumpkin
 1 Tbsp. pumpkin pie spice
 3 eggs
 1 cup **BREAKSTONE'S** or **KNUDSEN** Sour Cream
 1 square **BAKER'S** Semi-Sweet Baking Chocolate
 1 tsp. butter or margarine

PREHEAT oven to 350°F if using a silver 9-inch springform pan (or 325°F if using a dark 9-inch nonstick springform pan). Mix cookie crumbs and 2 Tbsp. butter; press firmly onto bottom of pan. Set aside.

BEAT cream cheese and sugar in large bowl with electric mixer on medium speed until well blended. Add pumpkin and pumpkin pie spice; mix well. Add eggs, 1 at a time, mixing on low speed after each addition just until blended. Pour over crust.

BAKE 50 to 55 min. or until center is almost set; cool slightly. Carefully spread sour cream over top of cheesecake. Run knife or metal spatula around rim of pan to loosen cake; cool before removing rim of pan.

PLACE chocolate and 1 tsp. butter in small microwaveable bowl. Microwave on MEDIUM 30 sec.; stir until chocolate is completely melted. Drizzle over cheesecake in spiral pattern. Starting at center of cheesecake, pull a toothpick through lines from center of cheesecake to outside edge of cheesecake to resemble a spider's web. Refrigerate 4 hours or overnight. Store leftover cheesecake in refrigerator.

PHILADELPHIA

Seasonal Desserts

Chocolate Cream Ornament Cake

Prep: 20 min. **Bake:** As directed. **Makes:** 16 servings, 1 slice each.

- 1 pkg. (2-layer size) chocolate cake mix
- 1 pkg. (4-serving size) **JELL-O** Chocolate Flavor Instant Pudding & Pie Filling
- 1 pkg. (8 oz.) **PHILADELPHIA** Cream Cheese, softened
- 1 cup powdered sugar
- 1½ cups thawed **COOL WHIP** Whipped Topping
- 1 **COMET** ice cream cone
- 1 piece red string licorice (2 inches)
  Decorating gel
  Colored sugar

PREHEAT oven to 350°F. Lightly grease 2 (9-inch) round cake pans. Prepare cake batter as directed on package. Blend in dry pudding mix. Pour evenly into prepared pans.

BAKE as directed on package. Cool 10 min.; remove from pans to wire racks. Cool completely. Meanwhile, beat cream cheese and powdered sugar in small bowl with electric mixer on medium speed until well blended. Add whipped topping; stir until well blended.

PLACE 1 of the cake layers on serving plate; spread with one-third of the cream cheese mixture. Cover with remaining cake layer. Spread top and side of cake with remaining cream cheese mixture. Poke 2 small holes in bottom of ice cream cone; insert ends of licorice into holes leaving small loop at top. Place cone next to cake to resemble ornament hanger. Decorate top of cake with decorating gel and colored sugar as desired. Store in refrigerator.

Easy Decorating Idea: For fun and easy patterns, place cookie cutters on top of cake and fill in shape with colored sugar.

White Chocolate-Peppermint Cheesecake

Prep: 15 min. plus refrigerating. **Bake:** 40 min. **Makes:** 16 servings, 1 piece each.

1½ cups **HONEY MAID** Graham Cracker Crumbs
 3 Tbsp. sugar
 ¼ cup (½ stick) butter, melted
 4 pkg. (8 oz. each) **PHILADELPHIA** Cream Cheese, softened
 1 cup sugar
 ¼ tsp. peppermint extract
 1 cup **BREAKSTONE'S** or **KNUDSEN** Sour Cream
 4 squares **BAKER'S** Premium White Baking Chocolate, melted
 4 eggs
 1 cup thawed **COOL WHIP** Whipped Topping
 16 starlight mints

PREHEAT oven to 325°F. Line 13×9-inch baking pan with foil, with ends of foil extending over sides of pan. Mix graham cracker crumbs, 3 Tbsp. sugar and the butter; press firmly onto bottom of prepared pan. Bake 10 min.

BEAT cream cheese, 1 cup sugar and the extract in large bowl with electric mixer on medium speed until well blended. Add sour cream and chocolate; mix well. Add eggs, 1 at a time, mixing on low speed after each addition just until blended. Pour over crust.

BAKE 40 min. or until center is almost set. Cool. Refrigerate at least 4 hours or overnight. Lift cheesecake from pan, using foil handles. Top each piece with a dollop of the whipped topping and a starlight mint just before serving. Store any leftover cheesecake in refrigerator.

Serving Suggestion: This is a great dessert to share at a holiday party. At 16 servings, there's enough for a crowd.

Seasonal Desserts

Cherries In The Snow

Prep: 10 min. **Makes:** 8 servings, about ⅔ cup each.

1 pkg. (8 oz.) **PHILADELPHIA** Cream Cheese, softened

½ cup sugar

2 cups thawed **COOL WHIP** Whipped Topping

1 can (20 oz.) cherry pie filling, divided

MIX cream cheese and sugar until well blended. Stir in whipped topping.

LAYER heaping 2 Tbsp. cream cheese mixture and 2 Tbsp. pie filling in each of 8 stemmed glasses or dessert dishes. Repeat layers. Store leftovers in refrigerator.

Substitute: Prepare as directed, using PHILADELPHIA Neufchâtel Cheese, ⅓ Less Fat than Cream Cheese and COOL WHIP LITE Whipped Topping.

Storage Know-How: Once thawed, refrigerate COOL WHIP Whipped Topping for up to 2 weeks or re-freeze.

Seasonal Desserts

PHILADELPHIA Snowmen Cookies

Prep: 20 min. **Bake:** 21 min. **Makes:** 22 servings, 2 cookies each.

- 1 pkg. (8 oz.) **PHILADELPHIA** Cream Cheese, softened
- 1 cup powdered sugar
- ¾ cup (1½ sticks) butter or margarine
- ½ tsp. vanilla
- 2 cups all-purpose flour
- ½ tsp. baking soda
- Suggested decorations: decorating gels, colored sprinkles, nonpareils and miniature peanut butter cups (optional)

PREHEAT oven to 325°F. Beat cream cheese, sugar, butter and vanilla with electric mixer on medium speed until well blended. Add flour and baking soda; mix well.

SHAPE dough into equal number of ½-inch and 1-inch diameter balls. (You should have about 44 of each size ball.) Using 1 small and 1 large ball for each snowman, place balls, slightly overlapping, on ungreased baking sheet. Flatten to ¼-inch thickness with bottom of glass dipped in additional flour. Repeat with remaining dough.

BAKE 19 to 21 minutes or until lightly browned. Cool on wire rack. Decorate as desired.

Size-Wise: A serving of these cookies along with a glass of low-fat milk is sure to be a hit as an after-school snack for your kids.

Jazz It Up: Decorate with decorating gels, colored sprinkles and nonpareils to resemble snowmen. Cut peanut butter cups in half. Place 1 candy half on top of each snowman for hat.

8

PHILADELPHIA 3-STEP Mini Cheesecake Basket

Prep: 10 min. **Total:** 2 hours 30 min. **Makes:** 12 servings.

2 pkg. (8 oz. each) **PHILADELPHIA** Cream Cheese, softened
½ cup sugar
½ tsp. vanilla
2 eggs
12 **NILLA** Wafers
1½ cups **BAKER'S ANGEL FLAKE** Coconut, tinted green
36 small jelly beans
12 pieces shoestring licorice (4 inches each)

PREHEAT oven to 350°F. Beat cream cheese, sugar and vanilla with electric mixer on medium speed until well blended. Add eggs; beat just until blended.

PLACE wafer on bottom of each of 12 paper-lined medium muffin cups. Spoon cream cheese mixture evenly over wafers.

BAKE 20 minutes or until centers are almost set. Cool. Refrigerate at least 2 hours. Top evenly with coconut and jelly beans just before serving. Bend each licorice piece, then insert both ends into each cheesecake to resemble the handle of a basket. Store leftover cheesecakes in refrigerator.

Size-Wise: These baskets are sure to be a hit at an Easter egg hunt. They are fun to make, and each basket is an easy portion to serve.

How To Tint Coconut: Place coconut and a few drops green food coloring in small resealable plastic bag. Seal bag. Shake bag gently until coconut is evenly tinted.

Variation: Omit NILLA Wafers. Prepare as directed, pouring batter evenly into 12 ready-to-use single-serve graham cracker crumb crusts.

Easy & Oven-Free

PHILADELPHIA No-Bake Chocolate Cherry Cheesecake

Prep: 10 min. plus refrigerating. **Makes:** 10 servings.

- 2 pkg. (8 oz. each) **PHILADELPHIA** Cream Cheese, softened
- 1 pkg. (4 oz.) **BAKER'S GERMAN'S** Sweet Chocolate, melted, cooled
- ⅓ cup sugar
- 1 tub (8 oz.) **COOL WHIP** Whipped Topping, thawed
- 1 **HONEY MAID** Graham Pie Crust (6 oz.)
- 1 can (21 oz.) cherry pie filling

BEAT cream cheese, chocolate and sugar in large bowl with electric mixer on medium speed until well blended. Gently stir in whipped topping.

SPOON into crust.

REFRIGERATE 3 hours or overnight. Top with pie filling just before serving. Store leftover cheesecake in refrigerator.

0

PHILADELPHIA

Easy & Oven-Free

Rocky Road No-Bake Cheesecake

Prep: 15 min. plus refrigerating. **Makes:** 10 servings, 1 slice each.

- 3 squares **BAKER'S** Semi-Sweet Baking Chocolate, divided
- 2 pkg. (8 oz. each) **PHILADELPHIA** Cream Cheese, softened
- ⅓ cup sugar
- ¼ cup milk
- 2 cups thawed **COOL WHIP** Whipped Topping
- ¾ cup **JET-PUFFED** Miniature Marshmallows
- ⅓ cup chopped **PLANTERS COCKTAIL** Peanuts
- 1 **OREO** Pie Crust (6 oz.)

MICROWAVE 1 of the chocolate squares in small microwaveable bowl on HIGH 1 min.; stir until chocolate is completely melted. Set aside.

BEAT cream cheese, sugar and milk in large bowl with electric mixer on medium speed until well blended. Add melted chocolate; mix well. Gently stir in whipped topping, marshmallows and peanuts. Coarsely chop remaining 2 chocolate squares; stir into cream cheese mixture. Spoon into crust.

REFRIGERATE 4 hours or until set. Garnish as desired. Store leftover cheesecake in refrigerator.

Easy & Oven-Free

PHILADELPHIA Blueberry No-Bake Cheesecake

Prep: 15 min. plus refrigerating. **Makes:** 16 servings, 1 piece each.

- 2 cups **HONEY MAID** Graham Cracker Crumbs
- 6 Tbsp. margarine, melted
- 1 cup sugar, divided
- 4 pkg. (8 oz. each) **PHILADELPHIA** Neufchâtel Cheese, ⅓ Less Fat than Cream Cheese, softened
- ½ cup blueberry preserves
  Grated peel from 1 lemon
- 1 pkg. (16 oz.) frozen blueberries, thawed, drained
- 1 tub (8 oz.) **COOL WHIP LITE** Whipped Topping, thawed

MIX graham crumbs, margarine and ¼ cup of the sugar; press firmly onto bottom of 13×9-inch pan. Refrigerate while preparing filling.

BEAT Neufchâtel cheese and remaining ¾ cup sugar in large bowl with electric mixer on medium speed until well blended. Add preserves and lemon peel, mix until blended. Stir in blueberries. Gently stir in whipped topping. Spoon over crust; cover.

REFRIGERATE 4 hours or until firm. Garnish as desired. Store leftovers in refrigerator.

How To Make It With Fresh Blueberries: Place 2 cups blueberries in small bowl with 2 Tbsp. sugar; mash with fork. Add to Neufchâtel cheese mixture; continue as directed.

Easy & Oven-Free

PHILADELPHIA No-Bake Mini Cheesecakes

Prep: 10 min. **Makes:** 12 servings.

- 1 pkg. (8 oz.) **PHILADELPHIA** Cream Cheese, softened
- ½ cup sugar
- 1 tub (8 oz.) **COOL WHIP** Whipped Topping, thawed
- 12 **OREO** Chocolate Sandwich Cookies
  - Multi-colored sprinkles (optional)

BEAT cream cheese and sugar until well blended. Gently stir in whipped topping.

PLACE cookies on bottom of 12 paper-lined muffin cups.

SPOON cream cheese mixture into muffin cups. Top with multi-colored sprinkles. Refrigerate until ready to serve.

Size-Wise: Sweets can add enjoyment to a balanced diet, but remember to keep tabs on portions.

Substitute: Substitute miniature chocolate chips for sprinkles.

PHILADELPHIA

Easy & Oven-Free

Lem'n Berry Cheesecake

Prep: 10 min. plus refrigerating. **Makes:** 8 servings.

- 1 pkg. (8 oz.) **PHILADELPHIA** Cream Cheese, softened
- ¼ cup **COUNTRY TIME** Lemonade Flavor Drink Mix
- 2 Tbsp. sugar
- ½ cup milk
- 2 cups thawed **COOL WHIP** Whipped Topping
- 1 **HONEY MAID** Graham Pie Crust (6 oz.)
- 1 cup assorted fresh berries

BEAT cream cheese, drink mix and sugar in large bowl until well blended. Gradually add milk, mixing until well blended. Gently stir in whipped topping.

SPOON into crust.

REFRIGERATE 1 hour or until ready to serve. Garnish with berries.

Great Substitute: Prepare as directed, using PHILADELPHIA Neufchâtel Cheese, ⅓ Less Fat than Cream Cheese and COOL WHIP LITE Whipped Topping.

Easy & Oven-Free

PHILADELPHIA Strawberry Fields No-Bake Cheesecake

Prep: 15 min. plus refrigerating. **Makes:** 16 servings, 1 piece each.

2 cups **HONEY MAID** Graham Cracker Crumbs

6 Tbsp. margarine, melted

1 cup sugar, divided

4 pkg. (8 oz. each) **PHILADELPHIA** Neufchâtel Cheese, ⅓ Less Fat than Cream Cheese, softened

½ cup strawberry preserves

1 pkg. (16 oz.) frozen strawberries, thawed, drained

1 tub (8 oz.) **COOL WHIP LITE** Whipped Topping, thawed

MIX graham crumbs, margarine and ¼ cup of the sugar; press firmly onto bottom of 13×9-inch pan. Refrigerate while preparing filling.

BEAT Neufchâtel cheese and remaining ¾ cup sugar in large bowl with electric mixer on medium speed until well blended. Add preserves; mix until blended. Stir in strawberries. Gently stir in whipped topping. Spoon over crust; cover.

REFRIGERATE 4 hours or until firm. Store leftovers in refrigerator.

How To Make It With Fresh Strawberries: Place 2 cups fresh strawberries in small bowl with additional 2 Tbsp. sugar; mash with fork. Add to Neufchâtel cheese mixture; continue as directed.

PHILADELPHIA

Easy & Oven-Free

OREO No-Bake Cheesecake

Prep: 15 min. plus refrigerating. **Makes:** 24 servings, 1 piece each.

- 1 pkg. (1 lb. 2 oz.) **OREO** Chocolate Sandwich Cookies, divided
- ¼ cup (½ stick) butter, melted
- 4 pkg. (8 oz. each) **PHILADELPHIA** Cream Cheese, softened
- ½ cup sugar
- 1 tsp. vanilla
- 1 tub (8 oz.) **COOL WHIP** Whipped Topping, thawed

LINE 13×9-inch pan with foil, with ends of foil extending over sides of pan. Coarsely chop 15 of the cookies; set aside. Finely crush remaining cookies; mix with butter. Press firmly onto bottom of prepared pan. Refrigerate while preparing filling.

BEAT cream cheese, sugar and vanilla in large bowl with electric mixer on medium speed until well blended. Gently stir in whipped topping and chopped cookies. Spoon over crust; cover.

REFRIGERATE 4 hours or until firm. Store leftover cheesecake in refrigerator.

Variation: Prepare as directed, using 1 pkg. (18 oz.) Golden Uh-Oh! OREO Chocolate Creme Sandwich Cookies.

PHILADELPHIA

Easy & Oven-Free

"Fruit Smoothie" No-Bake Cheesecake

Prep: 15 min. plus refrigerating. **Makes:** 16 servings, 1 piece each.

2 cups **HONEY MAID** Graham Cracker Crumbs

6 Tbsp. butter, melted

3 Tbsp. sugar

4 pkg. (8 oz. each) **PHILADELPHIA** Neufchâtel Cheese, ⅓ Less Fat than Cream Cheese, softened

¾ cup sugar

1 pkg. (12 oz.) frozen mixed berries (strawberries, raspberries, blueberries and blackberries), thawed, drained

1 tub (8 oz.) **COOL WHIP LITE** Whipped Topping, thawed

LINE 13×9-inch baking pan with foil, with ends of foil extending over sides of pan. Mix graham crumbs, butter and 3 Tbsp. sugar; press firmly onto bottom of prepared pan. Refrigerate while preparing filling.

BEAT Neufchâtel cheese and ¾ cup sugar in large bowl with electric mixer on medium speed until well blended. Add drained berries; beat on low speed just until blended. Gently stir in whipped topping. Spoon over crust; cover.

REFRIGERATE 4 hours or until firm. Use foil handles to remove cheesecake from pan before cutting into pieces to serve. Garnish as desired. Store leftover cheesecake in refrigerator.

Variation: Omit mixed frozen berries. Add 3 cups fresh mixed berries and additional ¼ cup sugar to Neufchâtel cheese mixture, mixing with electric mixer on medium speed until well blended.

PHILADELPHIA

Entrées

Stuffed Fiesta Burgers

Prep: 15 min. **Grill:** 9 min. **Makes:** 4 servings, 1 burger each.

- 1 lb. ground beef
- 1 pkg. (1¼ oz.) **TACO BELL® HOME ORIGINALS®** Taco Seasoning Mix
- ¼ cup **PHILADELPHIA** Chive & Onion Cream Cheese Spread
- ⅓ cup **KRAFT** Shredded Cheddar Cheese
- 4 hamburger buns, split, lightly toasted
- ½ cup **TACO BELL® HOME ORIGINALS®** Thick 'N Chunky Medium Salsa
- 1 avocado, peeled, pitted and cut into 8 slices

PREHEAT grill to medium heat. Mix meat and seasoning mix. Shape into 8 thin patties. Mix cream cheese spread and shredded cheese. Spoon about 2 Tbsp. of the cheese mixture onto center of each of 4 of the patties; top with second patty. Pinch edges of patties together to seal.

GRILL 7 to 9 min. on each side or until cooked through (160°F).

COVER bottom halves of buns with burgers. Top with salsa, avocado slices and top halves of buns.

TACO BELL® and HOME ORIGINALS® are trademarks owned and licensed by Taco Bell Corp.

Entrées

Zesty Chicken Pot Pie

Prep: 20 min. **Bake:** 25 min. **Makes:** 8 servings.

12 oz. (1½ pkg. [8 oz. each]) **PHILADELPHIA** Cream Cheese, cubed
½ cup chicken broth
3 cups chopped cooked chicken
2 pkg. (10 oz. each) frozen mixed vegetables, thawed
1 env. **GOOD SEASONS** Italian Salad Dressing & Recipe Mix
1 refrigerated ready-to-use refrigerated pie crust (½ of 15-oz. pkg.)

PREHEAT oven to 425°F. Place cream cheese in large saucepan. Add broth; cook on low heat until cream cheese is completely melted, stirring frequently with wire whisk. Stir in chicken, vegetables and salad dressing mix.

SPOON into 9-inch pie plate. Cover with pie crust; seal and flute edge. Cut several slits in crust to allow steam to escape. Place pie plate on baking sheet.

BAKE 20 to 25 min. or until golden brown.

Serving Suggestion: Serve with a mixed green salad and glass of fat-free milk.

Make Ahead: Prepare as directed except for baking. Wrap securely; freeze. When ready to bake, unwrap. Place strips of foil around edge to prevent over browning. Bake frozen pie at 425°F for 1 hour and 10 min. or until heated through.

Substitutes: Prepare as directed, using PHILADELPHIA Neufchâtel Cheese, ⅓ Less Fat than Cream Cheese, OR GOOD SEASONS Zesty Italian Dressing OR substituting turkey for the chicken.

PHILADELPHIA

Entrées

Italian Five-Cheese Chicken Roll-Ups

Prep: 10 min. **Cook:** 35 min. **Makes:** 4 servings.

- 1 cup **KRAFT** Finely Shredded Italian* Five Cheese Blend, divided
- 2 oz. (¼ of 8-oz. pkg.) **PHILADELPHIA** Cream Cheese, softened
- ¼ cup finely chopped green bell peppers
- ½ tsp. dried oregano leaves
- ¼ tsp. garlic salt
- 4 small boneless, skinless chicken breast halves (1 lb.), pounded to ¼-inch thickness
- 1 cup spaghetti sauce

PREHEAT oven to 400°F. Mix ½ cup of the shredded cheese, the cream cheese, peppers, oregano and garlic salt until well blended. Shape into 4 logs. Place 1 log on one of the short ends of each chicken breast; press into chicken lightly. Roll up each chicken breast tightly, tucking in ends of chicken around filling to completely enclose filling.

PLACE, seam-sides down, in 13×9-inch baking dish sprayed with cooking spray. Spoon spaghetti sauce evenly over chicken; cover with foil.

BAKE 30 min. or until chicken is cooked through (170°F). Remove foil; sprinkle chicken with remaining ½ cup shredded cheese. Bake an additional 3 to 5 min. or until cheese is melted.

*Made with quality cheeses crafted in the USA.

Family-Favorite Roast Chicken

Prep: 10 min. **Bake:** 1 hour 30 min. **Makes:** 8 servings.

- 1 (4½-lb.) roasting chicken
- ¼ tsp. black pepper
- ⅛ tsp. salt
- 1 medium lemon, washed
- 4 oz. (½ of 8-oz. pkg.) **PHILADELPHIA** Cream Cheese, softened
- 1 Tbsp. Italian seasoning
- ½ cup **KRAFT** Zesty Italian Dressing

PREHEAT oven to 350°F. Rinse chicken; pat dry with paper towel. Use the tip of a sharp knife to separate the chicken skin from the meat in the chicken breast and tops of the legs. Sprinkle chicken both inside and out with the pepper and salt. Place in 13×9-inch baking dish.

GRATE the lemon; mix the peel with cream cheese and Italian seasoning. Use a small spoon or your fingers to carefully stuff the cream cheese mixture under the chicken skin, pushing the cream cheese mixture carefully toward the legs, being careful to not tear the skin.

CUT the lemon in half; squeeze both halves into small bowl. Add dressing; beat with wire whisk until well blended. Drizzle evenly over chicken. Place the squeezed lemon halves inside the chicken cavity. Insert an ovenproof meat thermometer into thickest part of 1 of the chicken's thighs.

BAKE 1 hour 30 min. or until chicken is no longer pink in center (165°F), basting occasionally with the pan juices.

Entrées

Diner Special Meatloaf

Prep: 15 min. **Bake:** 55 min. **Makes:** 4 servings.

- 1 lb. lean ground beef
- ½ cup **KRAFT** Original Barbecue Sauce
- ½ cup dry bread crumbs
- 1 egg, lightly beaten
- 1¼ cups water
- ¾ cup milk
- 2 Tbsp. butter or margarine
- ½ tsp. salt
- 1½ cups instant potato flakes
- 3 oz. **PHILADELPHIA** Cream Cheese, cubed
- 2 **KRAFT** Singles

PREHEAT oven to 375°F. Mix meat, barbecue sauce, bread crumbs and egg. Shape into loaf in 12×8-inch baking dish.

BAKE 55 minutes. Meanwhile, bring water to boil in medium saucepan. Add milk, butter and salt; stir in potato flakes. Add cream cheese; stir until completely melted.

SPREAD potato mixture over meatloaf; top with Singles. Bake an additional 5 minutes or until Singles begin to melt.

Round Out The Meal: Serve with a steamed green vegetable, such as green beans, and a whole wheat roll.

Great Substitute: Substitute 1 pkg. (16 oz.) frozen LOUIS RICH Ground Turkey for the ground beef.

Special Extra: Garnish with chopped fresh chives just before serving.

PHILADELPHIA

Entrées

20-Minute Skillet Salmon

Prep: 10 min. **Cook:** 10 min. **Makes:** 4 servings.

1 Tbsp. oil
4 salmon fillets (1 lb.)
1 cup fat-free milk
½ cup (½ of 8-oz. tub) **PHILADELPHIA** Light Cream Cheese Spread
½ cup chopped cucumbers
2 Tbsp. chopped fresh dill

HEAT oil in large skillet on medium-high heat. Add salmon; cook 5 min. on each side or until salmon flakes easily with fork. Remove from skillet; cover to keep warm.

ADD milk and cream cheese spread to skillet; cook and stir until cream cheese spread is melted and mixture is well blended. Stir in cucumbers and dill.

RETURN salmon to skillet. Cook 2 min. or until heated through. Serve salmon topped with the cream cheese sauce.

Cooking Know-How: When salmon is done, it will appear opaque and flake easily with fork.

Food Facts: Check salmon fillets for bones before cooking by running fingers over surface. Small bumps are usually a sign of bones. Use tweezers to remove any bones.

Substitute: Substitute 2 tsp. dill weed for the 2 Tbsp. chopped fresh dill.

PHILADELPHIA

Entrées

Creamy Bow-Tie Pasta With Chicken And Broccoli

Prep: 10 min. **Cook:** 15 min. **Makes:** 6 servings, about 1½ cups each.

- 3 cups (8 oz.) farfalle (bow-tie pasta), uncooked
- 4 cups broccoli florets
- 3 Tbsp. **KRAFT** Roasted Red Pepper Italian with Parmesan Dressing
- 6 small boneless, skinless chicken breast halves (1½ lb.)
- 2 cloves garlic, minced
- 2 cups tomato-basil spaghetti sauce
- 4 oz. (½ of 8-oz. pkg.) **PHILADELPHIA** Neufchâtel Cheese, ⅓ Less Fat than Cream Cheese, cubed
- ¼ cup **KRAFT** 100% Grated Parmesan Cheese

COOK pasta as directed on package, adding broccoli to the cooking water for the last 3 min. of the pasta cooking time. Meanwhile, heat dressing in large nonstick skillet on medium heat. Add chicken and garlic; cook 5 min. Turn chicken over; continue cooking 4 to 5 min. or until chicken is cooked through (170°F).

DRAIN pasta mixture in colander; return to pan and set aside. Add spaghetti sauce and Neufchâtel cheese to chicken in skillet; cook on medium-low heat 2 to 3 min. or until Neufchâtel cheese is completely melted, mixture is well blended and chicken is coated with sauce, stirring occasionally. Remove chicken from skillet; keep warm. Add sauce mixture to pasta mixture; mix well. Transfer to six serving bowls.

CUT chicken crosswise into thick slices; fan out chicken over pasta mixture. Sprinkle evenly with Parmesan cheese.

Substitute: Prepare as directed, using whole wheat or multigrain pasta.

Entrées

Pasta Primavera Alfredo

Prep: 5 min. **Cook:** 15 min. **Makes:** 5 servings, 1¼ cups each.

4 oz. (½ of 8-oz. pkg.) **PHILADELPHIA** Cream Cheese, cubed

¾ cup milk

½ cup **KRAFT** Shredded Parmesan Cheese

¼ cup (½ stick) butter or margarine

¼ tsp. white pepper

¼ tsp. garlic powder

⅛ tsp. ground nutmeg

2 cups small broccoli florets

1 cup chopped carrots

1 pkg. (9 oz.) refrigerated fettuccine

PLACE cream cheese, milk, Parmesan cheese and butter in small saucepan; cook on medium-low heat until cream cheese is completely melted and mixture is well blended, stirring occasionally. Add pepper, garlic powder and nutmeg; stir until well blended.

MEANWHILE, add vegetables and pasta to 2½ qt. boiling water in large saucepan; cook 3 min. Drain.

TOSS pasta mixture with the cream cheese mixture.

PHILADELPHIA

Entrées

Chicken Enchiladas

Prep: 20 min. **Bake:** 20 min. **Makes:** 4 servings, 2 enchiladas each.

2 cups chopped cooked chicken or turkey

1 green bell pepper, chopped

4 oz. (½ of 8-oz. pkg.) **PHILADELPHIA** Cream Cheese, cubed

½ cup **TACO BELL® HOME ORIGINALS®** Thick 'N Chunky Salsa, divided

8 **TACO BELL® HOME ORIGINALS®** Flour Tortillas

¼ lb. (4 oz.) **VELVEETA** Pasteurized Prepared Cheese Product, cut into ½-inch cubes

1 Tbsp. milk

PREHEAT oven to 350°F. Mix chicken, green bell pepper, cream cheese and ¼ cup of the salsa in saucepan; cook on low heat until cream cheese is melted, stirring occasionally.

SPOON ⅓ cup of the chicken mixture down center of each tortilla; roll up. Place, seam-sides down, in lightly greased 13×9-inch baking dish. Place VELVEETA in small saucepan. Add milk; cook on low heat until VELVEETA is completely melted, stirring frequently. Pour over enchiladas; cover with foil.

BAKE 20 min. or until heated through. Top with remaining ¼ cup salsa.

TACO BELL® and HOME ORIGINALS® are trademarks owned and licensed by Taco Bell Corp.

Substitute: Prepare as directed, using PHILADELPHIA Neufchâtel Cheese, ⅓ Less Fat than Cream Cheese and VELVEETA Made With 2% Milk Reduced Fat Pasteurized Prepared Cheese Product.

Shortcut: Substitute 1 pkg. (6 oz.) OSCAR MAYER Oven Roasted Chicken Breast Cuts for the chopped cooked fresh chicken.